A DIARY
OF
PRIVATE PRAYER

A DIARY
OF
PRIVATE PRAYER

By
JOHN BAILLIE
D.D., D.Litt., S.T.D., LL.D.

*Professor of Divinity in the University
of Edinburgh; Chaplain to the King*

πρὸς τὸ δεῖν πάντοτε προσεύχεσθαι
αὐτοὺς καὶ μὴ ἐνκακεῖν

NEW YORK
CHARLES SCRIBNER'S SONS
1954

For
IAN

NOTE

Here are prayers for all the mornings and evenings of the month; and at the end of the book two prayers which, when any day falls on a Sunday, may be substituted for the others or else added to them. These prayers are to be regarded as aids; they are not intended to form the whole of the morning's or evening's devotions or to take the place of more individual prayers for oneself and others. On the blank left-hand pages such further petitions and intercessions may be noted down.

The prayers are suited to private use, not to the liturgical use of public worship.

* * * * * * * *

The little book has passed through many impressions since it was first published thirteen years ago, but in none of these were any changes made, apart from the correction of a few obvious misprints. The present edition has, however, been subjected to a certain amount of revision—largely in the light of comments received in correspondence.

1949

E TERNAL Father of my soul, let my first thought to-day be of Thee, let my first impulse be to worship Thee, let my first speech be Thy name, let my first action be to kneel before Thee in prayer.

For Thy perfect wisdom and perfect goodness:
For the love wherewith Thou lovest mankind:
For the love wherewith Thou lovest me:
For the great and mysterious opportunity of my life:
For the indwelling of Thy Spirit in my heart:
For the sevenfold gifts of Thy Spirit:
                    I praise and worship Thee, O Lord.

Yet let me not, when this morning prayer is said, think my worship ended and spend the day in forgetfulness of Thee. Rather from these moments of quietness let light go forth, and joy, and power, that will remain with me through all the hours of the day:
Keeping me chaste in thought:
Keeping me temperate and truthful in speech:
Keeping me faithful and diligent in my work:
Keeping me humble in my estimation of myself:
Keeping me honourable and generous in my dealings with others:
Keeping me loyal to every hallowed memory of the past:
Keeping me mindful of my eternal destiny as a child of Thine.

O God, who hast been the Refuge of my fathers through many generations, be my Refuge to-day in every time and circumstance of need. Be my Guide through all that is dark and doubtful. Be my Guard against all that threatens my spirit's welfare. Be my Strength in time of testing. Gladden my heart with Thy peace; through Jesus Christ my Lord. Amen.

O THOU who art from everlasting to everlasting, I would turn my thoughts to Thee as the hours of darkness and of sleep begin. O Sun of my soul, I rejoice to know that all night I shall be under the unsleeping eye of One who dwells in eternal light.

To thy care, O Father, I would now commend my body and my soul. All day Thou hast watched over me and Thy companionship has filled my heart with peace. Let me not go through any part of this night unaccompanied by Thee.

Give me sound and refreshing sleep:

Give me safety from all perils:

Give me in my sleep freedom from restless dreams:

Give me control of my thoughts, if I should lie awake:

Give me wisdom to remember that the night was made for sleeping, and not for the harbouring of anxious or fretful or shameful thoughts.

Give me grace, if as I lie abed I think at all, to think upon Thee.

My soul shall be satisfied as with marrow and fatness; and my mouth shall praise thee with joyful lips; when I remember thee upon my bed, and meditate on thee in the night watches.

To Thy care also, O Father, I would commend my friends, beseeching Thee to keep them safe in soul and body, and to be present in their hearts to-night as a Spirit of power and of joy and of restfulness. I pray for . . . and . . . . and . . . . I pray also for the wider circle of all my associates, my fellow workers, my fellow townsmen and all strangers within our gates; and the great world of men without, to me foreign and unknown, but dear to Thee; through Jesus Christ our common Lord. Amen.

TAKE ALL THE GOOD
THINGS ABOUT THEM
BACK IN GOD'S HANDS ON A DAILY
BASIS — TO REMIND YOU THEY ARE
NOT YOURS — BUT A TRUST GIVEN TO YOU BY GOD.

WHOM DO YOU
WRSHIP?

O GOD my Creator and Redeemer, I may not go forth to-day except Thou dost accompany me with Thy blessing. Let not the vigour and freshness of the morning, or the glow of good health, or the present prosperity of my undertakings, deceive me into a false reliance upon my own strength. All these good gifts have come to me from Thee. They were Thine to give and they are Thine also to curtail. They are not mine to keep; I do but hold them in trust; and only in continued dependence upon Thee, the Giver, can they be worthily enjoyed.

Let me then put back into Thine hand all that Thou hast given me, rededicating to Thy service all the powers of my mind and body, all my worldly goods, all my influence with other men. All these, O Father, are Thine to use as Thou wilt. All these are Thine, O Christ. All these are Thine, O Holy Spirit. Speak Thou in my words to-day, think in my thoughts, and work in all my deeds. And seeing that it is Thy gracious will to make use even of such weak human instruments in the fulfilment of Thy mighty purpose for the world, let my life to-day be the channel through which some little portion of Thy divine love and pity may reach the lives that are nearest to my own.

In Thy solemn presence, O God, I remember all my friends and neighbours, my fellow townsfolk, and especially the poor within our gates, beseeching Thee that Thou wouldst give me grace, so far as in me lies, to serve them in Thy name.

O blessed Jesus, who didst use Thine own most precious life for the redemption of Thy human brethren, giving no thought to ease or pleasure or worldly enrichment, but filling up all Thine hours and days with deeds of self-denying love, give me grace to-day to follow the road Thou didst first tread; and to Thy name be all the glory and the praise, even unto the end. Amen.

O FATHER in heaven, who didst fashion my limbs to serve Thee and my soul to follow hard after Thee, with sorrow and contrition of heart I acknowledge before Thee the faults and failures of the day that is now past. Too long, O Father, have I tried thy patience; too often have I betrayed the sacred trust Thou hast given me to keep; yet Thou art still willing that I should come to Thee in lowliness of heart, as now I do, beseeching Thee to drown my transgressions in the sea of Thine own infinite love.

My failure to be true even to my own accepted standards:

My self-deception in face of temptation:

My choosing of the worse when I know the better:

O Lord, forgive.

My failure to apply to myself the standards of conduct I demand of others:

My blindness to the suffering of others and my slowness to be taught by my own:

My complacence towards wrongs that do not touch my own case and my over-sensitiveness to those that do:

My slowness to see the good in my fellows and to see the evil in myself:

My hardness of heart towards my neighbours' faults and my readiness to make allowance for my own:

My unwillingness to believe that Thou hast called me to a small work and my brother to a great one:

O Lord, forgive.

Create in me a clean heart, O God; and renew a right spirit within me. Cast me not away from thy presence; and take not thy holy spirit from me. Restore unto me the joy of thy salvation, and give me the strength of a willing spirit. Amen.

LORD of my life, whose law I fain would keep, whose fellowship I fain would enjoy, and to whose service I would fain be loyal, I kneel before Thee as Thou sendest me forth to the work of another day.

For this new day I give Thee humble thanks: for its gladness and its brightness: for its long hours waiting to be filled with joyous and helpful labour: for its open doors of possibility: for its hope of new beginnings. Quicken in my heart, I beseech Thee, the desire to avail myself richly of this day's opportunity. Let me not break faith with any of yesterday's promises, nor leave unrepaired any of yesterday's wrongs. Let me see no fellow traveller in distress and pass by on the other side. Let me leave no height of duty behind me unattempted, nor any evil habit unassaulted. Where deed of mine can help to make this world a better place for men to live in, where word of mine can cheer a despondent heart or brace a weak will, where prayer of mine can serve the extension of Christ's Kingdom, there let me do and speak and pray

This day, O Lord—
     give me courtesy:
     give me meekness of bearing, with decision of character:
     give me longsuffering:
     give me charity:
     give me chastity:
     give me sincerity of speech:
     give me diligence in my allotted task.

O Thou who in the fullness of time didst raise up our Lord and Saviour Jesus Christ to enlighten our hearts with the knowledge of Thy love, grant me the grace to be worthy of His name. Amen.

O THOU most wise, most great, most holy, in wisdom and power and tender mercy Thou didst create me in Thine own image. Thou hast given me this life to live, Thou hast appointed my lot and determined the bounds of my habitation, Thou hast surrounded me with gracious and beneficent influences, Thou hast written Thy law within my heart.

And in my heart's most secret chamber Thou art now waiting to meet and speak with me, freely offering me Thy fellowship in spite of all my sinning. Let me now avail myself of this open road to peace of mind. Let me approach Thy presence humbly and reverently. Let me carry with me the spirit of my Lord and Master Jesus Christ. Let me leave behind me all fretfulness, all unworthy desires, all thoughts of malice towards my fellow men, all hesitancy in surrendering my will to Thine.

In Thy will, O Lord, is my peace.
In Thy love is my rest.
In Thy service is my joy.
Thou art all my heart's desire.
Whom have I in heaven but Thee?
And there is none upon earth that I desire besides
Thee.

In Thy presence, O God, I think not only of myself, but of others, my fellow men:
Of my friends, especially of . . . . and of . . . .:
Of those who to-day have worked or played with me:
Of those who are in sorrow:
Of those who are bearing the burdens of others:
Of those who are manning difficult stations or lonely outposts of Thy Kingdom:
O Thou who art the one God and Father of us all, be near to us all to-night and graciously keep watch over our souls. Hear my prayer for Jesus Christ's sake. Amen.

Salt Shakers and Dust Shakers
are the two compatible ?

SERMON
A LIFE
OF OPPOSITES
OR
UNCONDITIONAL
SURRENDER.

ALMIGHTY and eternal God,
    Thou art hidden from my sight:
Thou art beyond the understanding of my mind:
Thy thoughts are not as my thoughts:
Thy ways are past finding out.

Yet hast Thou breathed Thy Spirit into my life:
Yet hast Thou formed my mind to seek Thee:
Yet hast Thou inclined my heart to love Thee:
Yet hast Thou made me restless for the rest that is in
    Thee:
Yet hast Thou planted within me a hunger and thirst
    that make me dissatisfied with all the joys of earth.

O Lord God, I praise and magnify Thy name that
thus Thou hast set Thy seal upon my inmost being, not
leaving me to my own poor and petty selfhood or to the
sole empire of animal passion and desire, but calling me
to be an heir of Thine eternal Kingdom. I bless Thee
for that knocking at my heart's door that warns me of
Thy waiting presence. I bless Thee for Thy hand upon
my life, and for the sure knowledge that, however I may
falter and fail, yet underneath are Thine everlasting
arms.

O Thou who alone knowest what lies before me this
day, grant that in every hour of it I may stay close to
Thee. Let me be in the world, yet not of it. Let me use
this world without abusing it. If I buy, let me be as
though I possessed not. If I have nothing, let me be as
though possessing all things. Let me to-day embark on
no undertaking that is not in line with Thy will for my
life, nor shrink from any sacrifice which Thy will may
demand. Suggest, direct, control every movement of my
mind; for my Lord Christ's sake. Amen.

O THOU before whose eyes all human hearts lie bare and open, forbid that I should seek to hide from Thee anything that I have this day done or thought or imagined. What must for ever be hidden from the knowledge of others, that let me now openly acknowledge in Thy presence. What no proper shame kept me from committing, that let no false shame keep me now from confessing.

O Thou whose tender mercies are over all Thy works, humbly and sorrowfully I crave Thy forgiveness for the sins of this day;

> For every weakening and defiling thought to which my mind has given harbour:
> For every word spoken in hastiness or passion:
> For every failure of self-control:
> For every stumbling-block which by deed or example I have set in another's way:
> For every opportunity lost:
> For every blessing thanklessly received:
> For loitering feet and a procrastinating will:
> For this . . . .
> And this . . . .
> And this . . . .

And grant that, as the days go by, Thy Spirit may more and more rule in my heart, giving me victory over these and all other sinful ways.

To Thy loving guardianship, O holy Father, I commend all those who are dear to me, especially . . . . and . . . . Bless all those among whom my lot is cast, and grant them a satisfying sense of Thy reality and power. Be with all those who to-night are in any peril or distress. Be in every sore heart, in every stricken home, beside every bed of pain, giving to all the blessing of Thy peace. Amen.

I thank Thee that because God did first endure
so he can show me how to meet any temptation
or trial that I am called upon to face.

GOD of my forefathers, I cry unto Thee. Thou hast been the refuge of good and wise men in every generation. When history began, Thou wert the first enlightener of men's minds, and Thine was the Spirit that first led them out of their brutish estate and made them men. Through all the ages Thou hast been the Lord and giver of life, the source of all knowledge, the fountain of all goodness.

> The patriarchs trusted Thee and were not put to shame:
> The prophets sought Thee and Thou didst commit Thy word to their lips:
> The psalmist rejoiced in Thee and Thou wert **present** in their song:
> The apostles waited upon Thee and they were filled with Thy Holy Spirit:
> The martyrs called upon Thee and Thou wert with them in the midst of the flame:
> *This poor man cried, and the Lord heard him, and saved him out of all his troubles.*

O Thou who wast, and art, and art to come, I thank Thee that this Christian way whereon I walk is no untried or uncharted road, but a road beaten hard by the footsteps of saints, apostles, prophets, and martyrs. I thank Thee for the finger-posts and danger-signals with which it is marked at every turning and which may be known to me through the study of the Bible, and of all history, and of all the great literature of the world. Beyond all I give Thee devout and humble thanks for the great gift of Jesus Christ, the Pioneer of our faith. I praise Thee that Thou hast caused me to be born in an age and in a land which have known His name, and that I am not called upon to face any temptation or trial which He did not first endure.

Forbid it, Holy Lord, that I should fail to profit by these great memories of the ages that are gone by, or to enter into the glorious inheritance which Thou hast prepared for me; through Jesus Christ my Lord. Amen.

25

ALMIGHTY God, in this hour of quiet I seek communion with Thee. From the fret and fever of the day's business, from the world's discordant noises, from the praise and blame of men, from the confused thoughts and vain imaginations of my own heart, I would now turn aside and seek the quietness of Thy presence. All day long have I toiled and striven; but now, in stillness of heart and in the clear light of Thine eternity, I would ponder the pattern my life has been weaving.

May there fall upon me now, O God, a great sense of Thy power and Thy glory, so that I may see all earthly things in their true measure.

Let me not be ignorant of this great thing, that one day is with Thee as a thousand years and a thousand years as one day.

Give me now such understanding of Thy perfect holiness as will make an end of all pride in my own attainment.

Grant unto me now such a vision of Thine uncreated beauty as will make me dissatisfied with all lesser beauties.

Though earth and man were gone,
And suns and universes cease to be,
And Thou wert left alone,
Every existence would exist in Thee.

I am content, O Father, to leave my life in Thy hands, believing that the very hairs upon my head are numbered by Thee. I am content to give over my will to Thy control, believing that I can find in Thee a righteousness that I could never have won for myself. I am content to leave all my dear ones to Thy care, believing that Thy love for them is greater than my own. I am content to leave in Thy hands the causes of truth and of justice, and the coming of Thy Kingdom in the hearts of men, believing that my ardour for them is but a feeble shadow of Thy purpose. To Thee, O God, be glory for ever. Amen.

A SERIES ON JESUS

[HIS SENSITIVITY]

HIS SYMPATHY
HIS STEADFASTNESS OF PURPOSE

HIS SIMPLICITY
HIS SELF-DISCIPLINE
HIS SERENITY OF SPIRIT

O GOD, who hast proven Thy love for mankind by sending us Jesus Christ our Lord, and hast illumined our human life by the radiance of His presence, I give Thee thanks for this Thy greatest gift.

For my Lord's days upon earth:

For the record of His deeds of love:

For the words He spoke for my guidance and help:

For His obedience unto death:

For His triumph over death:

For the presence of His Spirit with me now:

I thank thee, O God.

Grant that the remembrance of the blessed Life that once was lived out on this common earth under these ordinary skies may remain with me in all the tasks and duties of this day. Let me remember—

His eagerness, not to be ministered unto, but to minister:

His sympathy with suffering of every kind:

His bravery in face of His own suffering:

His meekness of bearing, so that, when reviled, He reviled not again:

His steadiness of purpose in keeping to His appointed task:

His simplicity:

His self-discipline:

His serenity of spirit:

His complete reliance upon Thee, His Father in Heaven.

And in each of these ways give me grace to follow in His footsteps.

Almighty God, Father of our Lord Jesus Christ, I commit all my ways unto Thee. I make over my soul to Thy keeping. I pledge my life to Thy service. May this day be for me a day of obedience and of charity, a day of happiness and of peace. May all my walk and conversation be such as becometh the gospel of Christ. Amen.

O THOU who art the only origin of all that is good and fair and true, unto Thee I lift up my soul.

O God, let Thy Spirit now enter my heart.
> Now as I pray this prayer, let not any room within me be furtively closed to keep Thee out.

O God, give me power to follow after that which is good.
> Now as I pray this prayer, let there be no secret purpose of evil formed in my mind, that waits for an opportunity of fulfilment.

O God, bless all my undertakings and cause them to prosper.
> Now as I pray this prayer, let me not be still holding to some undertaking on which I dare not ask Thy blessing.

O God, give me chastity.
> Now as I pray this prayer, let me not say to myself secretly, *But not yet,* or, *But not overmuch.*

O God, bless every member of this household.
> Now as I pray this prayer, let me not still harbour in my heart a wrongful feeling of jealousy or bitterness or anger towards any of them.

O God, bless my enemies and those who have done me wrong.
> Now as I pray this prayer, let me not still cherish in my heart the resolve to requite them when occasion offers.

O God, let Thy Kingdom come on earth.
> Now as I pray this prayer, let me not be still intending to devote my own best hours and years to the service of lesser ends.

O Holy Spirit of God, as I rise from these acts of devotion, let me not return to evil thoughts and worldly ways, but let that mind be in me which was also in Christ Jesus. Amen.

O LORD and Maker of all things, from whose creative power the first light came forth, who didst look upon the world's first morning and see that it was good, I praise Thee for this light that now streams through my windows to rouse me to the life of another day.

I praise Thee for the life that stirs within me:
I praise Thee for the bright and beautiful world into which I go:
I praise Thee for earth and sea and sky, for scudding cloud and singing bird:
I praise Thee for the work Thou hast given me to do:
I praise Thee for all that Thou hast given me to fill my leisure hours:
I praise Thee for my friends:
I praise Thee for music and books and good company and all pure pleasures.

O Thou who Thyself art everlasting Mercy, give me a tender heart to-day towards all those to whom the morning light brings less joy than it brings to me:
Those in whom the pulse of life grows weak:
Those who must lie abed through all the sunny hours:
The blind, who are shut off from the light of day:
The overworked, who have no joy of leisure:
The unemployed, who have no joy of labour:
The bereaved, whose hearts and homes are desolate:
And grant Thy mercy on them all.

O Light that never fades, as the light of day now streams through these windows and floods this room, so let me open to Thee the windows of my heart, that all my life may be filled by the radiance of Thy presence. Let no corner of my being be unillumined by the light of Thy countenance. Let there be nothing within me to darken the brightness of the day. Let the Spirit of Him whose life was the light of men rule within my heart till eventide. Amen.

O ETERNAL Being, Thou livest in everlasting light; now, as the world's light fails, I seek the brightness of Thy presence.

Thou knowest no weariness; now, as my limbs grow heavy and my spirit begins to flag, I commit my soul to Thee.

Thou slumberest never; now, as I lie down to sleep, I cast myself upon Thy care.

Thou keepest watch eternally; now, when I lie helpless, I rely upon Thy love.

Before I sleep, O God, I would review this day's doings in the light of Thine eternity.

I remember with bitterness the duties I have shirked:
I remember with sorrow the hard words I have spoken:
I remember with shame the unworthy thoughts I have harboured.
Use these memories, O God, to save me, and then for ever blot them out.
I remember with gladness the beauties of the world today:
I remember with sweetness the deeds of kindness I have to-day seen done by others:
I remember with thankfulness the work Thou hast to-day enabled me to do and the truth Thou hast enabled me to learn.
Use these memories, O God, to humble me, and let them live for ever in my soul.

Before I sleep, I would for a moment rejoice in the loves and friendships wherewith Thou hast blessed my life. I rejoice in the dear memory of .... and of ....; knowing that, though they have passed into mystery, they have not passed beyond Thy love and care. I rejoice in my continued fellowship with .... and .... and ....; whom now, with my own soul, I entrust to Thy keeping through the hours of darkness. And for all who this night have not where to lay their heads or who, though lying down, cannot sleep for pain or for anxiety, I crave Thy pity in the name of our Lord Christ. Amen.

Father I thank Thee that Christ is my Light
& The Light of the world.

These Three belong to you Our God —
For Thine is: the kingdom
The Power
The Glory   for
ever

O GOD, who of Thy love and pity didst send us Jesus Christ for the illumination of our darkness, give me wisdom to profit by the words He spoke and grace to follow in the steps He trod.

Jesus Christ said, *When ye stand praying, forgive, if ye have ought against any.*

    O God, give me grace now so to do.

Jesus Christ said, *It is more blessed to give than to receive.*

    O God, give me grace to-day to think, not of what I can get, but of what I can give.

Jesus Christ said, *When thou doest alms, let not thy left hand know what thy right hand doeth.*

    O God, grant that what I give may be given without self-congratulation, and without thought of praise or reward.

Jesus Christ said, *Enter ye in at the strait gate.*

    O God, give me grace this day to keep to the narrow path of duty and honourable dealing.

Jesus Christ said, *Judge not.*

    O God, give me grace this day first to cast out the beam out of my own eye, before I regard the mote that is in my brother's eye.

Jesus Christ said, *What is a man profited, if he shall gain the whole world, and lose his own soul?*

    O God, give me grace so to live this day that, whatever else I lose, I may not lose my soul.

Jesus Christ said, *After this manner therefore pray ye* (and so, O Lord, I pray): *Our Father which art in heaven, Hallowed be thy name. Thy kingdom come. Thy will be done in earth, as it is in heaven. Give us this day our daily bread. And forgive us our debts, as we forgive our debtors. And lead us not into temptation, but deliver us from evil: For thine is the kingdom, the power, and the glory, for ever. Amen.*

O GOD, the Father of all mankind, I would bring before Thee to-night the burden of the world's life.
I would join myself to the great scattered company of
those who, in every corner of every land, are now cry-
ing out to Thee in their need. Hear us, O God, and look
in pity upon our manifold necessities, since Thou alone
art able to satisfy all our desire.

Especially do I commend to Thy holy keeping:
All who to-night are far from home and friends:
All who to-night must lie down hungry or cold:
All who suffer pain:
All who are kept awake by anxiety or suspense:
All who are facing danger:
All who must toil or keep watch while others sleep.
Give to them all, I pray, such a sense of Thy presence
with them as may turn their loneliness into comfort and
their trouble into peace.

O most loving God, who in the Person of Thy Son
Jesus Christ didst manifest Thy love to man by relieving
all manner of suffering and healing all manner of dis-
ease, grant Thy blessing, I pray, to all who in any
corner of the world are serving in Christ's name:
All ministers of the gospel of Christ:
All social workers:
All missionary workers abroad:
All doctors and nurses who faithfully tend the sick.
Accomplish through them Thy great purpose of good-
will to men, and grant them in their own hearts the joy
of Christ's most real presence.

And to me also, as I lie down, grant, O gracious
Father, the joy of a life surrendered to Christ's service
and the peace of sin forgiven through the power of His
Cross. Amen.

The correlation
between the two
needs exploring

HERE am I, O God, of little power and of mean estate, yet lifting up heart and voice to Thee before whom all created things are as dust and a vapour. Thou art hidden behind the curtain of sense, incomprehensible in Thy greatness, mysterious in Thine almighty power; yet here I speak with Thee familiarly as child to parent, as friend to friend. If I could not thus speak to Thee, then were I indeed without hope in the world. For it is little that I have power to do or to ordain. Not of my own will am I here, not of my own will shall I soon pass hence. Of all that shall come to me this day, very little will be such as I have chosen for myself. It is Thou, O hidden One, who dost appoint my lot and determine the bounds of my habitation. It is Thou who hast put power in my hand to do one work and hast withheld the skill to do another. It is Thou who dost keep in Thy grasp the threads of this day's life and who alone knowest what lies before me to do or to suffer. But because Thou art my Father, I am not afraid. Because it is Thine own Spirit that stirs within my spirit's inmost room, I know that all is well. What I desire for myself I cannot attain, but what Thou desirest in me Thou canst attain for me. The good that I would I do not, but the good that Thou willest in me, that Thou canst give me power to do.

Dear Father, take this day's life into Thine own keeping. Control all my thoughts and feelings. Direct all my energies. Instruct my mind. Sustain my will. Take my hands and make them skilful to serve Thee. Take my feet and make them swift to do Thy bidding. Take my eyes and keep them fixed upon Thine everlasting beauty. Take my mouth and make it eloquent in testimony to Thy love. Make this day a day of obedience, a day of spiritual joy and peace. Make this day's work a little part of the work of the Kingdom of my Lord Christ, in whose name these my prayers are said. Amen.

O MERCIFUL Father, who dost look down upon the weaknesses of Thy human children more in pity than in anger, and more in love than in pity, let me now in Thy holy presence inquire into the secrets of my heart.

Have I to-day done anything to fulfil the purpose for which Thou didst cause me to be born?

Have I accepted such opportunities of service as Thou in Thy wisdom hast set before my feet?

Have I performed without omission the plain duties of the day?

Give me grace to answer honestly, O God.

Have I to-day done anything to tarnish my Christian ideal of manhood?

Have I been lazy in body or languid in spirit?

Have I wrongfully indulged my bodily appetites?

Have I kept my imagination pure and healthy?

Have I been scrupulously honourable in all my business dealings?

Have I been transparently sincere in all I have professed to be, to feel, or to do?

Give me grace to answer honestly, O God.

Have I tried to-day to see myself as others see me?

Have I made more excuses for myself than I have been willing to make for others?

Have I, in my own home, been a peace-maker or have I stirred up strife?

Have I, while professing noble sentiments for great causes and distant objects, failed even in common charity and courtesy towards those nearest to me?

Give me grace to answer honestly, O God.

O Thou whose infinite love, made manifest in Jesus Christ, alone has power to destroy the empire of evil in my soul, grant that with each day that passes I may more and more be delivered from my besetting sins. Amen.

ie.

command me. Keeps me in mind.

O GOD, *thou art my God; early will I seek thee: my soul thirsteth for Thee, my flesh longeth for thee in a dry and thirsty land where no water is; to see thy power and thy glory, so as I have seen thee in the sanctuary. Because thy lovingkindness is better than life, my lips shall praise thee.*

Seven times a day do I praise thee, because of thy righteous judgments. Great peace have they which love thy law: and nothing shall offend them.

Wherewithal shall a young man cleanse his way? by taking heed thereto according to thy word.

Shew me thy ways, O Lord; teach me thy paths. Lead me in thy truth and teach me: for thou art the God of my salvation; on thee do I wait all the day.

Set a watch, O Lord, before my mouth; keep the door of my lips.

Order my steps in thy word; and let not any iniquity have dominion over me.

Lord, who shall abide in thy tabernacle? who shall dwell in thy holy hill? He that walketh uprightly, and worketh righteousness, and speaketh the truth in his heart. He that backbiteth not with his tongue, nor doeth evil to his neighbour, nor taketh up a reproach against his neighbour. In whose eyes a vile person is contemned; but he honoureth them that fear the Lord. He that sweareth to his own hurt, and changeth not. He that putteth not out his money to usury, nor taketh reward against the innocent. He that doeth these things shall never be moved.

Let the words of my mouth, and the meditation of my heart, be acceptable in thy sight, O Lord, my strength, and my redeemer. Amen.

ALMIGHTY and ever-blessed God, I thank Thee for the love wherewith Thou dost follow me all the days of my life. I thank Thee that Thou dost inform my mind with Thy divine truth and undergird my will with Thy divine grace. I thank Thee for every evidence of Thy Spirit's leading, and for all those little happenings which, though seeming at the time no more than chance, yet afterwards appear to me as part of Thy gracious plan for the education of my soul. O let me not refuse Thy leading or quench this light which Thou hast kindled within me, but rather let me daily grow in grace and in the knowledge of Jesus Christ my Lord and Master.

Yet I would not think only of myself or pray only for myself, as now I seek Thy presence. I would remember before Thee all my human brothers and sisters who need Thy help. Especially to-night I think—

of those who are faced by great temptations:

of those who are faced by tasks too great for their powers:

of those who stand in any valley of decision:

of those who are in debt or poverty:

of those who are suffering the consequences of misdeeds long ago repented of:

of those who, by reason of early surroundings, have never had a fair chance in life:

of all family circles broken by death:

of all missionaries of the Kingdom of Heaven in far-away corners of the earth:

of those who lift high the lamp of truth in lonely places:

of . . . . and . . . . and . . . .

Dear Father of mankind, make me the human channel, so far as in me lies, through which Thy divine love and pity may reach the hearts and lives of a few of those who are nearest to me. Amen.

O OMNIPRESENT One, beneath whose all-seeing eye our mortal lives are passed, grant that in all my deeds and purposes to-day I may behave with true courtesy and honour. Let me be just and true in all my dealings. Let no mean or low thought have a moment's place in my mind. Let my motives be transparent to all. Let my word be my bond. Let me take no unchivalrous advantage of anybody. Let me be generous in my judgment of others. Let me be disinterested in my opinions. Let me be loyal to my friends and magnanimous to my opponents. Let me face adversity with courage. Let me not ask or expect too much for myself.

Yet, O Lord God, let me not rest content with such an ideal of manhood as men have known apart from Christ. Rather let such a mind be in me as was in Him. Let me not rest till I come to the stature of His own fullness. Let me listen to Christ's question: *What do ye more than others?* And so may the threefold Christian graces of faith, hope, and love be more and more formed within me, until all my walk and conversation be such as becometh the gospel of Christ.

O Thou whose love to man was proven in the passion and death of Jesus Christ our Lord, let the power of His Cross be with me to-day. Let me love as He loved. Let my obedience be unto death. In leaning upon His Cross, let me not refuse my own; yet in bearing mine, let me bear it by the strength of His.

O Thou who hast set the solitary in families, I crave Thy heavenly blessing also for all the members of this household, all my neighbours, and all my fellow citizens. Let Christ rule in every heart and His law be honoured in every home. Let every knee be bent before Him and every tongue confess that He is Lord. Amen.

O MERCIFUL heart of God, in true penitence and contrition I would now open my heart to Thee. Let me keep nothing hidden from Thee, while I pray. Humbling as the truth about myself may be, let me yet take courage to speak it in Thy presence. What I did not think shame to commit, that let me not think shame to confess. And in Thy wisdom use this pain of confession as a means to make me hate the sins confessed.

I confess to the sin of laziness in this....and this....:

I confess to the sin of vanity in this....and this....:

I confess to this .... and this .... indulgence of the flesh:

I confess to the habit of falsehood in this .... and this ....:

I confess to this .... and this .... dishonesty:

I confess to this .... and this .... uncharitable word:

I confess to having harboured this .... and this .... evil thought:

I confess to this .... and this .... wrong direction my life has been taking:

I confess to this .... and this .... lapse from faithful religious practice.

O Thou whose love can be in the heart of man as a fire to burn up all that is shameful and evil, let me now lay hold upon Thy perfect righteousness and make it mine own. Blot out all my transgressions and let my sins be covered. Make me to feel Thine hand upon my life, cleansing me from the stain of past misdeeds, loosing me from the grip of evil habits, strengthening me in new habits of pure-heartedness, and guiding my footsteps in the way of eternal life. Lead me in battle, O God, against my secret sins. Fence round my life with a rampart of pure aspiration. And let Christ be formed in my heart through faith. All this I ask for His holy name's sake. Amen.

O ETERNAL God, though Thou art not such as I can
see with my eyes or touch with my hands, yet grant
me this day a clear conviction of Thy reality and power.
Let me not go forth to my work believing only in the
world of sense and time, but give me grace to understand that the world I cannot see or touch is the most
real world of all. My life to-day will be lived in time,
but eternal issues will be concerned in it. The needs of
my body will be clamant, but it is for the needs of my
soul that I must care most. My business will be with
things material, but behind them let me be aware of
things spiritual. Let me keep steadily in mind that the
things that matter are not money or possessions, not
houses or lands, not bodily comfort or bodily pleasure;
but truth and honour and meekness and helpfulness and
a pure love of Thyself.

For the power Thou hast given me to lay hold of
     things unseen:
For the strong sense I have that this is not my home:
For my restless heart which nothing finite can satisfy:
                    I give Thee thanks, O God.
For the invasion of my soul by Thy Holy Spirit:
For all human love and goodness that speak to me of
     Thee:
For the fullness of Thy glory outpoured in Jesus
     Christ:
                    I give Thee thanks, O God.

I, a pilgrim of eternity, stand before Thee, O eternal
One. Let me not seek to deaden or destroy the desire
for Thee that disturbs my heart. Let me rather yield myself to its constraint and go where it leads me. Make me
wise to see all things to-day under the form of eternity,
and make me brave to face all the changes in my life
which such a vision may entail: through the grace of
Christ my Saviour. Amen.

O THOU in whose boundless being are laid up all treasures of wisdom and truth and holiness, grant that through constant fellowship with Thee the true graces of Christian character may more and more take shape within my soul:

The grace of a thankful and uncomplaining heart:

The grace to await Thy leisure patiently and to answer Thy call promptly:

The grace of courage, whether in suffering or in danger:

The grace to endure hardness as a good soldier of Jesus Christ:

The grace of boldness in standing for what is right:

The grace of preparedness, lest I enter into temptation:

The grace of bodily discipline:

The grace of strict truthfulness:

The grace to treat others as I would have others treat me:

The grace of charity, that I may refrain from hasty judgement:

The grace of silence, that I may refrain from hasty speech:

The grace of forgiveness towards all who have wronged me:

The grace of tenderness towards all who are weaker than myself:

The grace of steadfastness in continuing to desire that Thou wilt do as now I pray.

And now, O God, give me a quiet mind, as I lie down to rest. Dwell in my thoughts until sleep overtake me. Let me rejoice in the knowledge that, whether awake or asleep, I am still with Thee. Let me not be fretted by any anxiety over the lesser interests of life. Let no troubled dreams disturb me, so that I may awake refreshed and ready for the tasks of another day. And to Thy Name be all the glory. Amen.

O HIDDEN Source of life, let me now meditate upon the great and gracious plan by which Thou hast brought it to pass that a mortal man like me should look up to Thee and call Thee Father.

In the beginning Thou, the Uncreated,
Making all things out of nothing:
Space and time and material substance:
All things that creep and fly, the beasts of the forest, the fowls of the air, the fish of the sea:
And at last man, in Thine own image, to have fellowship with Thyself:
Then when, in the corruption and disobedience of his heart, that image had been defaced:
A gracious design for its restoration through the gift of Thine only-begotten Son:
New life in Him, and a new access to Thy holy presence.

O hidden love of God, whose will it is that all created spirits should live everlastingly in pure and perfect fellowship with Thyself, grant that in my life to-day I may do nothing to defeat this Thy most gracious purpose. Let me keep in mind how Thy whole creation groans and travails, waiting for the perfect appearing of the sons of God; and let me welcome every influence of Thy Spirit upon my own that may the more speedily make for that end. When Thou dost knock at my heart's door, let me not keep Thee standing without but welcome Thee with joy and thanksgiving. Let me harbour nothing in my heart that might embarrass Thy presence; let me keep no corner of it closed to Thine influence. Do what Thou wilt with me, O God; make of me what Thou wilt, and change me as Thou wilt, and use me as Thou wilt, both now and in the larger life beyond; through Jesus Christ our Lord. Amen.

O HEAVENLY Father, give me a heart like the heart of Jesus Christ, a heart more ready to minister than to be ministered unto, a heart moved by compassion towards the weak and the oppressed, a heart set upon the coming of Thy kingdom in the world of men.

I would pray to-night, O God, for all those sorts and conditions of men to whom Jesus Christ was wont to give especial thought and care;
 For those lacking food or drink or raiment:
 For the sick and all who are wasted by disease:
 For the blind:
 For the maimed and lame:
 For lepers:
 For prisoners:
 For those oppressed by any injustice:
 For the lost sheep of our human society:
 For fallen women:
 For all lonely strangers within our gates:
 For the worried and anxious:
 For those who are living faithful lives in obscurity:
 For those who are fighting bravely in unpopular causes:
 For all who are labouring diligently in Thy vineyard.

Grant, O Father, that Thy lovingkindness in causing my own lines to fall in pleasant places may not make me less sensitive to the needs of others less privileged, but rather more incline me to lay their burdens upon my own heart. And if any adversity should befall myself, then let me not brood upon my own sorrows, as if I alone in the world were suffering, but rather let me busy myself in the compassionate service of all who need my help. Thus let the power of my Lord Christ be strong within me and His peace invade my spirit. Amen.

WHAt DOES
it MEAN TO

HAVE
A
HEART

O THOU who indwellest in our poor and shabby human life, lifting it now and then above the dominance of animal passion and greed, allowing it to shine with the borrowed lights of love and joy and peace, and making it a mirror of the beauties of a world unseen, grant that my part in the world's life to-day may not be to obscure the splendour of Thy presence but rather to make it more plainly visible to the eyes of my fellow men.

Let me stand to-day—
> for whatever is pure and true and just and good:
> for the advancement of science and education and true learning:
> for the redemption of daily business from the blight of self-seeking:
> for the rights of the weak and the oppressed:
> for industrial co-operation and mutual help:
> for the conservation of the rich traditions of the past:
> for the recognition of new workings of Thy Spirit in the minds of the men of my own time:
> for the hope of yet more glorious days to come.

To-day, O Lord—
> let me put right before interest:
> let me put others before self:
> let me put the things of the spirit before the things of the body:
> let me put the attainment of noble ends above the enjoyment of present pleasures:
> let me put principle above reputation:
> let me put Thee before all else,

O Thou the reflection of whose transcendent glory did once appear unbroken in the face of Jesus Christ, give me to-day a heart like His—a brave heart, a true heart, a tender heart, a heart with great room in it, a heart fixed on Thyself; for His name's sake. Amen.

O DIVINE Love who dost everlastingly stand outside the closed doors of the souls of men, knocking ever and again, wilt Thou not now give me grace to throw open all my soul's doors? To-night let every bolt and bar be drawn that has hitherto robbed my life of air and light and love.

Give me an open ear, O God, that I may hear Thy voice calling me to high endeavour. Too often have I been deaf to the appeals Thou hast addressed to me, but now give me courage to answer, *Here am I, send me.* And when any one of Thy children, my human brothers, cries out in need, give me then an open ear to hear in that cry Thy call to service.

Give me an open mind, O God, a mind ready to receive and to welcome such new light of knowledge as it is Thy will to reveal to me. Let not the past ever be so dear to me as to set a limit to the future. Give me courage to change my mind, when that is needed. Let me be tolerant to the thoughts of others and hospitable to such light as may come to me through them.

Give me open eyes, O God, eyes quick to discover Thine indwelling in the world which Thou hast made. Let all lovely things fill me with gladness and let them uplift my mind to Thine everlasting loveliness. Forgive all my past blindness to the grandeur and glory of nature, to the charm of little children, to the sublimities of human story, and to all the intimations of Thy presence which these things contain.

Give me open hands, O God, hands ready to share with all who are in want the blessings with which Thou hast enriched my life. Deliver me from all meanness and miserliness. Let me hold my money in stewardship and all my worldly goods in trust for Thee; to whom now be all honour and glory. Amen.

KEEPING THINGS IN TRUE PERS...

MY RELATIONSHIP TO THE WORLD

Though mortal, I am immortal

Though corruptible I am incorruptible

In this world but not of it

Possessing nothing, yet having all things

Only a place of sojourn (just passing thru)

———— To a kingdom not built with hands

The vanity of the temporal vs. the
glory of the eternal

A world centered not on myself but in you

O GOD who art from eternity unto eternity, and art not at one time in one place because all times and places are in Thee, I would now seek to understand my destiny as a child of Thine. Here I stand, weak and mortal, amid the immensities of nature. But blessed be Thou, O Lord God, that Thou hast made me in Thine own likeness and hast breathed into me the breath of Thine own life. Within this poor body Thou hast set a spirit that is akin to Thine own Spirit. Within this corruptible Thou hast planted incorruption and within this mortal immortality. So from this little room and this short hour I can lift up my mind beyond all time and space to Thee, the uncreated One, until the light of Thy countenance illumines all my life.

Let me keep in mind that my mortal body is but the servant of my immortal soul:

Let me keep in mind how uncertain is my hold upon my bodily life:

Let me remember that here I have no continuing city, but only a place of sojourn and a time of testing and of training:

Let me use this world as not abusing it:

Let me be in this world but not of it:

Let me be as having nothing yet possessing all things:

Let me understand the vanity of the temporal and the glory of the eternal:

Let my world be centred not in myself but in Thee:

Almighty God, who didst raise from the dead our Lord Jesus Christ and didst set Him at Thy right hand in glory everlasting, I thank Thee for this hope of immortality with which through many ages Thou hast cheered and enlightened the souls of Thy saints, and which Thou didst most surely seal through the same Jesus Christ our Lord. Amen.

O GOD of mercy, who so carest for me as if Thou hadst none else to care for, yet carest for all even as Thou carest for me, I commend to Thee my own needs but also the needs of all this world of men to which I belong.

Remember me in Thy mercy, O God, and keep me by Thy grace. Forgive the scanty use I have made to-day of the talents Thou hast entrusted to my keeping. Cover up the poverty of my service by the fullness of Thine own divine resource. Yet grant also that, as day succeeds day, I may be so strengthened by Thy help that my service may grow less unworthy and my sins less grievous. May Christ more and more reign in my heart and purify my deeds.

Remember also in Thy mercy all the sons of men. Let the whole earth be filled with Thy praise and made glad by the knowledge of Thy name. Let there fall upon all mankind a sense of Thine excellent greatness. Let the nations fear Thee. Let Thy glory rule over every court and market-place. Let Thy law be honoured in every home. Redeem the whole world's life, O God, and transform it utterly through the power of the Holy Cross.

O Thou who dost graciously condescend to use our poor human efforts towards the attainment of Thy blessed purpose, I pray for all who are devoting their lives to the evangelization of the world. I pray for all missionaries in foreign lands, especially . . . I pray for all who are working in the cause of peace and understanding between the nations, and for all who are striving to break down the dividing walls between Jew and Gentile, bond and free, and to make all one in Christ Jesus. Encourage them with the joy of Thy presence; and kindle in me the urgent desire to further and support their labours as far as in me lies; through Jesus Christ. Amen.

HE MAKES THE RIGHT DECISIONS
HE JUDGES WITH RIGHT JUDGEMENT
THATS HOW THE WORLD LEARNS THE
MEANING OF RIGHTEOUSNESS.

Wᴵᵀʜ *my soul have I desired thee in the night; yea, with my spirit within me will I seek thee early; for when thy judgments are in the earth, the inhabitants of the world will learn righteousness.*

Give me, O God, this day a strong and vivid sense that Thou art by my side. In multitude and solitude, in business and leisure, in my downsitting and in my uprising, may I ever be aware of Thine accompanying presence. By Thy grace, O God, I will go nowhere this day where Thou canst not come, nor court any companionship that would rob me of Thine. By Thy grace I will let no thought enter my heart that might hinder my communion with Thee, nor let any word come from my mouth that is not meant for Thine ear. So shall my courage be firm and my heart be at peace.

> *I steadier step*
> *When I recall*
> *That though I slip*
> *Thou dost not fall.*

O Thou Desire of all nations, in the knowledge of whose love and power there is salvation for all the peoples of the earth, hasten the day, I beseech Thee, when all men shall acknowledge Thee as Lord over all. Hasten the day when our earthly society shall become the kingdom of Christ. Hasten the day when Thy presence and the strong hand of Thy purpose shall be found not only in the hearts of a few wise and brave men but throughout the broad land, in court and council-chamber, in workshop and market-place, in the city and in the fields. And whatever I myself can do, give me grace this day to begin; through Jesus Christ. Amen.

O THOU whose eternal love for our weak and strug-
gling race was most perfectly shown forth in the
blessed life and death of Jesus Christ our Lord, enable
me now so to meditate upon my Lord's passion that,
having fellowship with Him in His sorrow, I may also
learn the secret of His strength and peace.

I remember Gethsemane:
I remember how Judas betrayed Him:
I remember how Peter denied Him:
I remember how *they all forsook Him and fled*:
I remember the scourging:
I remember the crown of thorns:
I remember how they spat upon Him:
I remember how they smote Him on the head with a
    reed:
I remember His pierced hands and feet:
I remember His agony on the Cross:
I remember His thirst:
I remember how He cried, *My God, my God, why hast
    Thou forsaken me?*

> *We may not know, we cannot tell,*
> *What pains He had to bear;*
> *But we believe it was for us*
> *He hung and suffered there.*

Grant, O most gracious God, that I who now kneel
before Thee may be embraced in the great company of
those to whom life and salvation have come through the
Cross of Christ. Let the redeeming power that has
flowed from His sufferings through so many generations
flow now into my soul. Here let me find forgiveness of
sin. Here let me learn to share with Christ the burden
of the suffering of the world. Amen.

O Lord, do I really want to know you present with me throughout this day?

I WILL NEVER UNDERSTAND YOUR WAYS,

LORD - I NEED NOT UNDERSTAND YOUR WAYS. BUT GIVE ME THE GRACE TO UNDERSTAND WHAT I NEED TO KNOW.

A LMIGHTY God, who art ever present in the world without me, in my spirit within me, and in the unseen world above me, let me carry with me through this day's life a most real sense of Thy power and Thy glory.

O God without me, forbid that I should look to-day upon the work of Thy hands and give no thought to Thee the Maker. Let the heavens declare Thy glory to me and the hills Thy majesty. Let every fleeting loveliness I see speak to me of a loveliness that does not fade. Let the beauty of earth be to me a sacrament of the beauty of holiness made manifest in Jesus Christ my Lord.

O God within me, give me grace to-day to recognize the stirrings of Thy Spirit within my soul and to listen most attentively to all that Thou hast to say to me. Let not the noises of the world ever so confuse me that I cannot hear Thee speak. Suffer me never to deceive myself as to the meaning of Thy commands; and so let me in all things obey Thy will, through the grace of Jesus Christ my Lord.

O God above me, God who dwellest in light unapproachable, teach me, I beseech Thee, that even my highest thoughts of Thee are but dim and distant shadowings of Thy transcendent glory. Teach me that if Thou art in nature, still more art Thou greater than nature. Teach me that if Thou art in my heart, still more art Thou greater than my heart. Let my soul rejoice in Thy mysterious greatness. Let me take refuge in the thought that Thou art utterly beyond me, beyond the sweep of my imagination, beyond the comprehension of my mind, Thy judgements being unsearchable and Thy ways past finding out.

O Lord, hallowed be Thy name. Amen.

I BLESS Thee, O most holy God, for the unfathomable love whereby Thou hast ordained that spirit with spirit can meet and that I, a weak and erring mortal, should have this ready access to the heart of Him who moves the stars.

With bitterness and true compunction of heart I acknowledge before Thee the gross and selfish thoughts that I so often allow to enter my mind and to influence my deeds.

I confess, O God—

that often I let my mind wander down unclean and forbidden ways:

that often I deceive myself as to where my plain duty lies:

that often, by concealing my real motives, I pretend to be better than I am:

that often my honesty is only a matter of policy:

that often my affection for my friends is only a refined form of caring for myself:

that often my sparing of my enemy is due to nothing more than cowardice:

that often I do good deeds only that they may be seen of men, and shun evil ones only because I fear they may be found out.

O holy One, let the fire of Thy love enter my heart, and burn up all this coil of meanness and hypocrisy, and make my heart as the heart of a little child.

Give me grace, O God, to pray now with pure and sincere desire for all those with whom I have had to do this day. Let me remember now my friends with love and my enemies with forgiveness, entrusting them all, as I now entrust my own soul and body, to Thy protecting care; through Jesus Christ. Amen.

O THOU whose eternal presence is hid behind the veil of nature, informs the mind of man, and was made flesh in Jesus Christ our Lord, I thank Thee that He has left me an example that I should follow in His steps.

Jesus Christ said, *Lay not up for yourselves treasures upon earth, but lay up for yourselves treasures in heaven.*

O God, incline my heart to follow in this way.

Jesus Christ said, *Seek ye first the kingdom of God and his righteousness.*

O God, incline my heart to follow in this way.

Jesus Christ said, *Do good and lend, hoping for nothing again.*

O God, incline my heart to follow in this way.

Jesus Christ said, *Love your enemies.*

O God, incline my heart to follow in this way.

Jesus Christ said, *Watch and pray, that ye enter not into temptation.*

O God, incline my heart to follow in this way.

Jesus Christ said, *Fear not, only believe.*

O God, incline my heart to follow in this way.

Jesus Christ said, *Except ye turn again and become as little children, ye shall not enter into the kingdom of heaven.*

O God, incline my heart to follow in this way.

Jesus Christ said, *Ask, and it shall be given you; seek, and ye shall find; knock, and it shall be opened unto you.*

O God, incline my heart to follow in this way.

Our Father, which art in heaven, hallowed be thy name; thy kingdom come; thy will be done; in earth as it is in heaven. Give us this day our daily bread. And forgive us our trespasses, as we forgive them that trespass against us. And lead us not into temptation; but deliver us from evil; for thine is the kingdom, the power, and the glory, for ever and ever. Amen.

O DIVINE Father, whose mercy ever awaits those who return unto Thee in true lowliness and contrition of heart, hear now one humble suppliant who needs Thy help. Bravely did I set out this morning upon the life of a new day; now I lie down ashamed and burdened with memories of things undone that ought to have been done and things done that ought not to have been done. Bring to me afresh, O God, Thy healing and cleansing power, so that again I may lay hold of the salvation which Thou hast offered to me through Jesus Christ my Lord.

For my deceitful heart and crooked thoughts:
For barbed words spoken deliberately:
For thoughtless words spoken hastily:
For envious and prying eyes:
For ears that rejoice in iniquity and rejoice not in the truth:
For greedy hands:
For wandering and loitering feet:
For haughty looks:
   Have mercy upon me, O God.

If we say that we have no sin, we deceive ourselves.

Almighty God, Spirit of purity and grace, in asking Thy forgiveness I cannot claim a right to be forgiven but only cast myself upon Thine unbounded love.
I can plead no merit or desert:
I can plead no extenuating circumstance:
I cannot plead the frailty of my nature:
I cannot plead the force of the temptations I encounter:
I cannot plead the persuasions of others who led me astray:
I can only say, For the sake of Jesus Christ Thy Son my Lord. Amen.

EVER READY —

BLESSED be Thou, most gracious God, that again Thou hast brought light out of darkness and caused the morning to appear! Blessed be Thou that Thou dost send me forth, in health and vigour, to the duties and doings of another day! Go with me, I beseech Thee, through all the sunlit hours, and so protect me from every evil way that, when evening comes, I need not hide my head in shame.

O Thou who hast so graciously called me to be Thy servant, I would hold myself in readiness to-day for Thy least word of command. Give me the spirit, I pray Thee, to keep myself in continual training for the punctual fulfilment of Thy most holy will.

Let me keep the edges of my mind keen:
Let me keep my thinking straight and true:
Let me keep my passions in control:
Let me keep my will active:
Let me keep my body fit and healthy:
Let me remember Him whose meat it was to do the will of Him that sent Him.

O Lord of the vineyard, I beg Thy blessing upon all who truly desire to serve Thee by being diligent and faithful in their several callings, bearing their due share of the world's burden, and going about their daily tasks in all simplicity and uprightness of heart.

For all who tend flocks or till the soil:
For all who work in factories or in mines:
For all who buy and sell in the market-place:
For all who labour with their brains:
For all who labour with their pens:
For all who tend the hearth:

> Dear Lord, I pray.

In Thy great mercy save us all from the temptations that do severally beset us, and bring us to everlasting life, by the power of the Holy Cross. Amen.

L ET me now rejoice, O most gracious God, in the love Thou hast shown to our poor human race, opening up to us a way whereby we might be delivered from our sin and foolishness.

O God the Father, I praise the great and holy love whereby, when we had utterly gone astray, Thou didst diligently seek us out and save us, sending Thy well-beloved Son to suffer and to die that we might be restored to the fellowship of Thy children.

O God the Son, I praise the great and holy love whereby Thou didst humble Thyself for my sake and for the sake of my brethren, consenting to share our common life, to dwell in the midst of all our sin and shame, to endure all the bitterness of Thy most blessed Passion, and at the last to die upon the Cross, that we might be released from our bondage and enter with Thee into the glorious liberty of the children of God.

O God the Holy Spirit, I praise the great and holy love whereby Thou dost daily shed abroad in my unworthy heart the peace and joy of sin forgiven, making me a partaker with all the saints in the blessings of my Lord's Incarnation, of His Passion and Crucifixion, and of His Resurrection and Ascension to the Father's right hand on high.

O holy and blessed Trinity, let me now so dwell in the mystery of this heavenly love that all hatred and malice may be rooted out from my heart and life. Let me love Thee, as Thou didst first love me; and in loving Thee let me love also my neighbour; and in loving Thee and my neighbour in Thee let me be saved from all false love of myself; and to Thee, Father, Son, and Holy Spirit, be all glory and praise for ever. Amen.

Almighty God, who of Thine infinite wisdom hast ordained that I should live my life within these narrow bounds of time and circumstance, let me now go forth into the world with a brave and trustful heart. It has pleased Thee to withhold from me a perfect knowledge; therefore deny me not the grace of faith by which I may lay hold of things unseen. Thou hast given me little power to mould things to my own desire; therefore use Thine own omnipotence to bring Thy desires to pass within me. Thou hast willed it that through labour and pain I should walk the upward way; be Thou then my fellow traveller as I go.

Let me face what Thou dost send with the strength Thou dost supply:

When Thou prosperest my undertakings, let me give heed that Thy word may prosper in my heart:

When Thou callest me to go through the dark valley, let me not persuade myself that I know a way round:

Let me not refuse any opportunity of service which may offer itself to-day, nor fall prey to any temptation that may lie in wait for me:

Let not the sins of yesterday be repeated in the life of to-day, nor the life of to-day set any evil example to the life of to-morrow.

O God of my forefathers, who hast in every age enlightened the souls of the faithful, I thank Thee for the gift of racial memory whereby the storied past still lives with us to-day. I thank Thee for the lives of the saints, and for the help that I may win from their example. I thank Thee for the memory of....and....and....; for apostles, prophets, and martyrs; but most for the Incarnation of Thy dear Son, in whose name these my prayers are said. Amen.

Lord, *I cry unto thee: make haste unto me; give ear unto my voice, when I cry unto thee. Let my prayer be set forth before thee as incense; and the lifting up of my hands as the evening sacrifice.*

O Lord, open thou my lips, and my mouth shall shew forth thy praise.

Bless the Lord, O my soul, and forget not all his benefits:
who forgiveth all thine iniquities;
who healeth all thy diseases;
who redeemeth thy life from destruction;
who crowneth thee with lovingkindness and tender mercies;
who satisfieth thy mouth with good things; so that thy youth is renewed like the eagle's.

Who can understand his errors? cleanse thou me from secret faults. Keep back thy servant from presumptuous sins; let them not have dominion over me: then shall I be upright, and I shall be innocent from the great transgression.

Have mercy upon me, O God, according to thy lovingkindness: according unto the multitude of thy tender mercies, blot out my transgressions. Wash me throughly from mine iniquity, and cleanse me from my sin. For I acknowledge my transgressions: and my sin is ever before me.

Be thou my strong habitation, whereunto I may continually resort.

So will I sing praise unto thy name for ever, that I may daily perform my vows.

I will both lay me down in peace, and sleep: for thou, Lord, only makest me dwell in safety. Amen.

WHAT DOES it MEAN TO BE FILLED WITH THE HOLY SPIRIT?

WHAT it MEANS TO RESOICE IN THE SPIRIT'S MYSTERIOUS COMPANIONSHIP.

INSPIRES MYTHOUGHTS

INVADES MHY IMAGINATION
PERVADES

SUGGESTS ALL MY DECISIONS

W/ PRAYER IS THAT YOU WILL LODGE IN MY WILL'S MOST
INWARD CITADEL & AND ORDER ALL MY DOINGS

O HOLY Spirit of God, visit now this soul of mine, and tarry within it until eventide. Inspire all my thoughts. Pervade all my imaginations. Suggest all my decisions. Lodge in my will's most inward citadel and order all my doings. Be with me in my silence and in my speech, in my haste and in my leisure, in company and in solitude, in the freshness of the morning and in the weariness of the evening; and give me grace at all times to rejoice in Thy mysterious companionship.

My heart an altar, and Thy love the flame.

Accompany me to-day, O Spirit invisible, in all my goings, but stay with me also when I am in my own home and among my kindred. Forbid that I should fail to show to those nearest to me the sympathy and consideration which Thy grace enables me to show to others with whom I have to do. Forbid that I should refuse to my own household the courtesy and politeness which I think proper to show to strangers. Let charity to-day begin at home.

Leave me not, O gracious Presence, in such hours as I may to-day devote to the reading of books or of newspapers. Guide my mind to choose the right books and, having chosen them, to read them in the right way. When I read for profit, grant that all I read may lead me nearer to Thyself. When I read for recreation, grant that what I read may not lead me away from Thee. Let all my reading so refresh my mind that I may the more eagerly seek after whatsoever things are pure and fair and true.

Let me have a special sense of Thy nearness to me, O God, in such times as I may be able to devote to prayer, to any public exercise of worship, or to the receiving of the Blessed Sacrament; through Jesus Christ my Lord. Amen.

Disappointments,   "THIS IS NOT MY
Adversity   HOME"
Calamity : ALL   FOR THOSE OF US WHO
SERVVE TO REMIND   BECOME DEMENSIA Victims.
US - "THIS NOT MY HOME"

That NI ENHANCES THEY READLY
EVER SOTISFIES - REMIND ME: THIS IS NOT MY HOME.

O THOU Creator of all things that are, I lift up my
heart in gratitude to Thee for this day's happiness:
For the mere joy of living:
For all the sights and sounds around me:
For the sweet peace of the country and the pleasant
    bustle of the town:
For all things bright and beautiful and gay:
For friendship and good company:
For work to perform and the skill and strength to per-
    form it:
For a time to play when the day's work was done,
    and for health and a glad heart to enjoy it.

Yet let me never think, O eternal Father, that I am
here to stay. Let me still remember that I am a stranger
and pilgrim on the earth. *For here we have no continuing city, but we seek one to come.* Preserve me by Thy
grace, good Lord, from so losing myself in the joys of
earth that I may have no longing left for the purer joys
of heaven. Let not the happiness of this day become a
snare to my too worldly heart. And if, instead of happiness, I have to-day suffered any disappointment or defeat, if there has been any sorrow where I had hoped
for joy, or sickness where I had looked for health, give
me grace to accept it from Thy hand as a loving re-
minder that this is not my home.

I thank Thee, O Lord, that Thou hast so set eternity
within my heart that no earthly thing can ever satisfy
me wholly. I thank Thee that every present joy is so
mixed with sadness and unrest as to lead my mind up-
wards to the contemplation of a more perfect blessedness. And above all I thank Thee for the sure hope and
promise of an endless life which Thou hast given me in
the glorious gospel of Jesus Christ my Lord. Amen.

I THANK YOU FOR THE
Church:

    it's consciousness

    cheering me in lonlinec

    Protecting me in company

    strengthening me against
    Temptation

   encouraging me To all

     suita charitable deeds

O LORD my God, I would kneel before Thee in lowly adoration ere I set out to face the tasks and interests of another day. I thank Thee for the blessed assurance that I shall not be called upon to face them alone or in my own strength, but shall at all times be accompanied by Thy presence and fortified by Thy grace. I thank Thee that through all our human life there run the footprints of our Lord and Saviour Jesus Christ, who for our sakes was made flesh and tasted all the changes of our mortal lot. I thank Thee for the many spiritual presences with which I shall to-day be surrounded as I go about my work. For the heavenly host above, for the saints who rest from their labours, for patriarchs, prophets, and apostles, for the noble army of martyrs, for all holy and humble men of heart, for my own dear departed friends, especially . . . . and . . . ., I bless and adore Thy great name. I rejoice, O God, that Thou hast called me to be a member of the Church of Christ. Let the consciousness of this holy fellowship follow me whithersoever I go, cheering me in loneliness, protecting me in company, strengthening me against temptation and encouraging me to all just and charitable deeds.

O Lord Jesus Christ, who didst bid Thy disciples to shine as lights in a dark world, in shame and contrition of heart do I acknowledge before Thee the many faults and weaknesses of which we are guilty who in this generation represent Thy Church before the world; and especially do I acknowledge my own part in the same. Forgive me, I beseech Thee, the feebleness of my witness, the smallness of my charity, and the slackness of my zeal. Make me to be a more worthy follower of Him who cared for the poor and the oppressed, and who could never see disease without seeking to heal it or any kind of human need without turning aside to help.

Let Thy power, O Christ, be in us all, to share the world's suffering and redress its wrongs. Amen.

Now, O Lord, when the day's work is done, I turn once more to Thee. From Thee all comes, in Thee all lives, in Thee all ends. In the morning I set out with Thy blessing, all day Thou hast upheld me by Thy grace, and now I pray that Thou wouldst grant me rest and peace. I would cast all my cares upon Thee and leave to Thee the issue of my labour. Prosper, I beseech Thee, all that has been done to-day in accordance with Thy will, and forgive all that has been done amiss. What good I have done to-day, graciously own and further; and if I have done any harm, annul and overrule it by Thine almighty power.

O Lord, I remember before Thee to-night all the workers of the world:
Workers with hand or brain:
Workers in cities or in the fields:
Men who go forth to toil and women who keep house:
Employers and employees:
Those who command and those who obey:
Those whose work is dangerous:
Those whose work is monotonous or mean:
Those who can find no work to do:
Those whose work is the service of the poor or the healing of the sick or the proclamation of the gospel of Christ at home or in foreign places.

O Christ, who camest not to be ministered unto but to minister, have mercy upon all who labour faithfully to serve the common good. O Christ, who didst feed the hungry multitude with loaves and fishes, have mercy upon all who labour to earn their daily bread. O Christ, who didst call unto Thyself all them that labour and are heavy laden, have mercy upon all whose work is beyond their strength. And to Thee, with the Father and the Holy Spirit, be all the glory and the praise. Amen.

GOD's THREE G's
GOOD
GREAT
GRACIOUS

Holy Father, from whom alone all good proceedeth, let the Christian graces of faith, hope, and charity be every day more firmly established within me.

O God, I believe—

that Thou rulest all things in wisdom and in righteousness:

that Thou hast called me to be Thy loyal servant:

that Thou dost rightfully demand of me complete subservience to Thy will:

that in Jesus Christ Thou hast shown me a way of salvation whereby I may be delivered from my sins:

that if I truly repent, Thou art willing to pardon and save me.

O God, I hope—

for the continuance of Thy daily mercies:

for the lessening of sin's hold upon my will:

for my growth in grace and in true holiness from day to day:

for a more perfect holiness, when earthly days are done:

for a day when I shall know even as also I am known.

O God, I love Thee—

who Thyself art love:

who in love didst create me and in love dost still preserve me:

who didst so love me as to send Thy Son to suffer and to die that I might live with Thee:

who hast commanded me to show my love to Thee by loving my neighbour for Thy sake.

Help Thou mine unbelief, O God, give me greater patience in my hope, and make me more constant in my love. In loving let me believe and in believing let me love; and in loving and in believing let me hope for a more perfect love and a more unwavering faith, through Jesus Christ my Lord. Amen.

O EVERLASTING God, let the light of Thine eternity now fall upon my passing days. O holy God, let the light of Thy perfect righteousness fall upon my sinful ways. O most merciful God, let the light of Thy love pierce to the most secret corners of my heart and overcome the darkness of sin within me.

Am I living as my conscience approves?

Am I demanding of others a higher standard of conduct than I demand of myself?

Am I taking a less charitable view of the failings of my neighbours than I am of my own?

Am I standing in public for principles which I do not practise in private?

> Let my answer before Thee be truthful, O God.

Do I ever allow bodily appetites to take precedence over spiritual interests?

To which do I give the benefit of the doubt, when my course is not clear?

Do I ever allow the thought of my own gain to take precedence over the interests of the community?

To which do I give the benefit of the doubt, when my course is not clear?

> Let my answer before Thee be truthful, O God.

Am I, in my daily life, facing the stress of circumstance with manliness and courage?

Am I grateful for my many blessings?

Am I allowing my happiness to be too much dependent on money? On business success? Or on the good opinion of others?

Is the sympathy I show to others who are in trouble commensurate with the pity I would expend on myself, if the same things happened to me?

> Let my answer before Thee be truthful, O God.

Create in me a clean heart, O God; and renew a right spirit within me. Through Jesus Christ. Amen.

O GOD, ever blessed, who hast given me the night for rest and the day for labour and service, grant that the refreshing sleep of the night now past may be turned to Thy greater glory in the life of the day now before me. Let it breed no slothfulness within me, but rather send me to more diligent action and more willing obedience.

Teach me, O God, so to use all the circumstances of my life to-day that they may bring forth in me the fruits of holiness rather than the fruits of sin.

Let me use disappointment as material for patience:
Let me use success as material for thankfulness:
Let me use suspense as material for perseverance:
Let me use danger as material for courage:
Let me use reproach as material for longsuffering:
Let me use praise as material for humility:
Let me use pleasures as material for temperance:
Let me use pains as material for endurance.

O Lord Jesus Christ, who for the joy that was set before Thee didst endure the Cross, despising the shame, and art now set down at the right hand of the throne of God, let me consider Thee who didst endure such contradiction of sinners against Thyself, lest I be wearied and faint in my mind.

> *'But that toil shall make thee*
> *Some day all Mine own,—*
> *And the end of sorrow*
> *Shall be near My throne.'*

Holy God, I would remember before Thee all my friends and those of my own household, especially.... and...., beseeching Thee that in Thy great love Thou wouldst keep them also free from sin, controlling all their deeds this day in accordance with Thy most perfect will. Amen.

Now unto Thee, O heavenly Father, be all praise and glory that day by day Thou dost richly fill my life with various blessings:

A home to share, kindred to love, and friends to cherish:

A place to fill and a work to do:

A green world to live in, blue skies above me, and pure air to breathe:

Healthy exercise and simple pleasures:

My race's long history to remember and its great men to follow:

Good books to read and many arts and crafts to delight in:

So much that is worth knowing and the skill and science to know it:

Those high thoughts that sometimes fill my mind and come I know not whence:

Many happy days, and that inward calm that Thou givest me in days of gloom:

The peace, passing understanding, that comes from Thine indwelling in my soul:

The faith that looks through death and the hope of a larger life beyond the grave.

I thank Thee, O Lord God, that though with liberal hand Thou hast at all times showered Thy blessings upon our human kind, yet in Jesus Christ Thou hast done greater things for us than Thou ever didst before:

Making home sweeter and friends dearer:

Turning sorrow into gladness and pain into the soul's victory:

Robbing death of its sting:

Robbing sin of its power:

Making peace more peaceful and joy more joyful and faith and hope more secure. Amen.

O GOD of the ages, grant that I, who am the heir of all the ages, may not fail to profit by the heavenly wisdom which in time past Thou didst grant to Thy servants.

A wise man wrote,
The World is too much with us; late and soon,
Getting and spending, we lay waste our powers.
> O God, give me grace to profit by this word.

A wise man wrote,
Our wills are ours to make them Thine.
> O God, give me grace to profit by this word.

A wise king said,
Nothing for me is too early or too late which is in due time for Thee.
> O God, give me grace to profit by this word.

A wise man said,
Expect great things from God, attempt great things for God.
> O God, give me grace to profit by this word.

A wise man said,
In His Will is our peace.
> O God, give me grace to profit by this word.

A wise woman said,
The divine moment is the present moment.
> O God, give me grace to profit by this word.

A wise woman said,
He asks too much to whom God is not sufficient.
> O God, give me grace to profit by this word.

A wise man prayed,
Give what Thou commandest, and command what Thou wilt.
> O God, give me grace to pray this prayer.

A wise man prayed,
My past life hide; my future guide.
> *(Quod vixi tege, quod vivam rege.)*
> O God, give me grace to pray this prayer.

Grant, O Father, that I may go about this day's business with an ever-present remembrance of the great traditions wherein I stand and the great cloud of witnesses which at all times surround me, that thereby I may be kept from evil ways and inspired to high endeavour. So keep me until evening in the might of Jesus Christ my Lord. Amen.

HOLY God, to whose service I long ago dedicated my soul and life, I grieve and lament before Thee that I am still so prone to sin and so little inclined to obedience:

So much attached to the pleasures of sense, so negligent of things spiritual:

So prompt to gratify my body, so slow to nourish my soul:

So greedy for present delight, so indifferent to lasting blessedness:

So fond of idleness, so indisposed for labour:

So soon at play, so late at prayer:

So brisk in the service of self, so slack in the service of others:

So eager to get, so reluctant to give:

So lofty in my profession, so low in my practice:

So full of good intentions, so backward to fulfil them:

So severe with my neighbours, so indulgent with myself:

So eager to find fault, so resentful at being found fault with:

So little able for great tasks, so discontented with small ones;

So weak in adversity, so swollen and self-satisfied in prosperity:

So helpless apart from Thee, and yet so little willing to be bound to Thee.

O merciful heart of God, grant me yet again Thy forgiveness. Hear my sorrowful tale and in Thy great mercy blot it out from the book of Thy remembrance. Give me faith so to lay hold of Thine own holiness and so to rejoice in the righteousness of Christ my Saviour that, resting on His merits rather than on my own, I may more and more become conformed to His likeness, my will becoming one with His in obedience to Thine. All this I ask for His holy name's sake. Amen.

O THOU to whom I owe the gift of this day's life, give to me also, I beseech Thee, the spirit to use it as I ought. Forbid that I should stain the brightness of the morning with any evil thought or darken the noontide with any shameful deed. Let Thy Holy Spirit breathe into my heart to-day all pure and heavenly desires. Let Thy truth inform my mind. Let Thy justice and right-eousness make a throne within me and rule my errant will. Let Christ be formed in me, and let me learn of Him all lowliness of heart, all gentleness of bearing, all modesty of speech, all helpfulness of action, and promptness in the doing of my Father's will.

O Thou who compassest the whole earth with Thy most merciful favour and willest not that any of Thy children should perish, I would call down Thy blessing to-day upon all who are striving towards the making of a better world. I pray, O God, especially—

for all who are valiant for truth:
for all who are working for purer and juster laws:
for all who are working for peace between the nations:
for all who are engaged in healing disease:
for all who are engaged in the relief of poverty:
for all who are engaged in the rescue of the fallen:
for all who are working towards the restoration of the broken unity of Thy Holy Church:
for all who preach the gospel:
for all who bear witness to Christ in foreign lands:
for all who suffer for righteousness' sake.

Cast down, O Lord, all the forces of cruelty and wrong. Defeat all selfish and worldly-minded schemes, and prosper all that is conceived among us in the spirit of Christ and carried out to the honour of His blessed name. Amen.

G RACIOUS God, I seek Thy presence at the close of
another day, beseeching Thee to create a little pool
of heavenly peace within my heart ere I lie down to
sleep. Let all the day's excitements and anxieties now
give place to a time of inward recollection, as I wait
upon Thee and meditate upon Thy love.

Give me to-night, dear Father, a deeper sense of gratitude to Thee for all Thy mercies. Thy goodness to me
has been wonderful. At no moment of the day have I
lacked Thy gracious care. At no moment have I been
called upon to stand in my own strength alone. When I
was too busy with my petty concerns to remember Thee,
Thou with a universe to govern wert not too busy to remember me.

I am bitterly ashamed, O God, that always I must be
confessing to Thee my forgetfulness of Thee, the feebleness of my love for Thee, the fitfulness and listlessness
of my desire. How many plain commandments of Thine
have I this day disobeyed! How many little services of
love have I withheld from Thee, O Christ, in that I
withheld them from the least of these Thy brethren
with whom I have had to do!

Dear Lord, if at this evening hour I think only of myself and my own condition and my own day's doings
and my day's record of service, then I can find no peace
before I go to sleep, but only bitterness of spirit and
miserable despair. Therefore, O Father, let me think
rather of Thee and rejoice that Thy love is great enough
to blot out all my sins. And, O Christ, Thou Lamb of
God, let me think of Thee, and lean upon Thy heavenly
righteousness, taking no pleasure in what I am before
Thee but only in what Thou art for me and in my stead.
And, O Holy Spirit, do Thou think within me, and so
move within my mind and will that as the days go by I
may be more and more conformed to the righteousness
of Jesus Christ my Lord; to whom be glory for ever.
Amen.

TWENTY-SEVENTH DAY   MORNING

ALL THINGS WORK TOGETHER FOR GOOD FOR
THEM WHO LOVE GOD "
HOW DOES TEMPORAL SORROW
BUILD UP ETERNAL JOYS

BURDENS
OF THE HEART

GRANT, O most gracious God, that I may carry with me through this day's life the remembrance of the sufferings and death of Jesus Christ my Lord.

For Thy fatherly love shown forth in Jesus Christ Thy well-beloved Son:

For His readiness to suffer for our sakes:

For the redemptive passion that filled His heart:

I praise and bless Thy holy name.

For the power of His Cross in the history of the world since He came:

For all who have taken up their own crosses and have followed Him:

For the noble army of martyrs and for all who are willing to die that others may live:

For all suffering freely chosen for noble ends, for pain bravely endured, for temporal sorrows that have been used for the building up of eternal joys:

I praise and bless Thy holy name.

O Lord my God, who dwellest in pure and blessed serenity beyond the reach of mortal pain, yet lookest down in unspeakable love and tenderness upon the sorrows of earth, give me grace, I beseech Thee, to understand the meaning of such afflictions and disappointments as I myself am called upon to endure. Deliver me from all fretfulness. Let me be wise to draw from every dispensation of Thy providence the lesson Thou art minded to teach me. Give me a stout heart to bear my own burdens. Give me a willing heart to bear the burdens of others. Give me a believing heart to cast all burdens upon Thee.

Glory be to Thee, O Father, and to Thee, O Christ, and to Thee, O Holy Spirit, for ever and ever. Amen.

> *I falter where I firmly trod,*
> *And falling with my weight of cares*
> *Upon the great world's altar-stairs*
> *That slope thro' darkness up to God,*
> *I stretch lame hands of faith, and grope . . . .*

ETERNAL God, who hast been the hope and joy of many generations, and who in all ages hast given men the power to seek Thee and in seeking to find Thee, grant me, I pray Thee, a clearer vision of Thy truth, a greater faith in Thy power, and a more confident assurance of Thy love.

When the way seems dark before me, give me grace to walk trustingly:

When much is obscure to me, let me be all the more faithful to the little that I can clearly see:

When the distant scene is clouded, let me rejoice that at least the next step is plain:

When what Thou art is most hidden from my eyes, let me still hold fast to what Thou dost command:

When insight falters, let obedience stand firm:

What I lack in faith let me repay in love.

O infinite God, the brightness of whose face is often shrouded from my mortal gaze, I thank Thee that Thou didst send Thy Son Jesus Christ to be a light in a dark world. O Christ, Thou Light of Light, I thank Thee that in Thy most holy life Thou didst pierce the eternal mystery as with a great shaft of heavenly light, so that in seeing Thee we see Him whom no man hath seen at any time.

And if still I cannot find Thee, O God, then let me search my heart and know whether it is not rather I who am blind than Thou who art obscure, and I who am fleeing from Thee rather than Thou from me; and let me confess these my sins before Thee and seek Thy pardon in Jesus Christ my Lord. Amen.

LET me now go forth, O Lord my God, to the work of another day, still surrounded by Thy wonderful lovingkindnesses, still pledged to Thy loyal service, still standing in Thy strength and not my own.

Let me to-day be a Christian not only in my words
    but also in my deeds:
Let me follow bravely in the footsteps of my Master,
    wherever they may lead:
Let me be hard and stern with myself:
Let there be no self-pity or self-indulgence in my life
    to-day:
Let my thinking be keen, my speech frank and open,
    and my action courageous and decisive.

I would pray, O Lord, not only for myself but for all the household to which I belong, for all my friends and all my fellow workers, beseeching Thee to include them all in Thy fatherly regard. I pray also—

for all who will to-day be faced by any great decision:
for all who will to-day be engaged in settling affairs of
    moment in the lives of men and nations:
for all who are moulding public opinion in our time:
for all who write what other people read:
for all who are holding aloft the lamp of truth in a
    world of ignorance and sin:
for all whose hands are worn with too much toil, and
    for the unemployed whose hands to-day fall idle:
for those who have not where to lay their head.

O Christ my Lord, who for my sake and my brethren's didst forgo all earthly comfort and fullness, forbid it that I should ever again live unto myself. Amen.

O UNAPPROACHABLE Light, how can I fold these guilty hands before Thee? How can I pray to Thee with lips that have spoken false and churlish words?

A heart hardened with vindictive passions:
An unruly tongue:
A fretful disposition:
An unwillingness to bear the burdens of others:
An undue willingness to let others bear my burdens:
High professions joined to low attainments:
Fine words hiding shabby thoughts:
A friendly face masking a cold heart:
Many neglected opportunities and many uncultivated talents:
Much love and beauty unappreciated and many blessings unacknowledged:
       All these I confess to Thee, O God.

I thank Thee, O loving Father, that, holy and transcendent as Thou art, Thou hast through all the ages shown Thyself to be accessible to the prayers of erring mortals such as I; and especially I praise Thy name that in the gospel of Jesus Christ Thou hast opened up a new and living way into Thy presence, making Thy mercy free to all who have nothing else to plead. Let me now find peace of heart by fleeing from myself and taking refuge in Thee. Let despair over my miserable sins give place to joy in Thine adorable goodness. Let depression of mind make way for renewed zeal and for the spirit of service. So let me lie down to-night thinking, not of myself and my own affairs, or of my own hopes and fears, or even of my own sins in Thy sight, but of others who need Thy help and of the work that I can do for their sakes in the vineyard of Thy world. Amen.

ALMIGHTY and most merciful Father, whose power and whose love eternally work together for the protection of Thy children, give me grace this day to put my trust in Thee.

O Father, I pray—

for faith to believe that Thou dost rule the world in truth and righteousness:

for faith to believe that if I seek first Thy Kingdom and righteousness, Thou wilt provide for all my lesser needs:

for faith to take no anxious thought for the morrow, but to believe in the continuance of Thy past mercies:

for faith to see Thy purpose of love unfolding itself in the happenings of this time:

for faith to be calm and brave in face of such dangers as may meet me in the doing of my duty:

for faith to believe in the power of Thy love to melt my hard heart and swallow up my sin:

for faith to put my own trust in love rather than in force, when other men harden their hearts against me:

for faith to believe in the ultimate victory of Thy Holy Spirit over disease and death and all the powers of darkness:

for faith to profit by such sufferings as Thou dost call upon me to endure:

for faith to leave in Thy hands the welfare of all my dear ones, especially....and....

O Thou in whom all my fathers trusted and were not put to confusion, rid my heart now of all vain anxieties and paralysing fears. Give me a cheerful and buoyant spirit, and peace in doing Thy will; for Christ's sake. Amen.

O GOD, immortal, eternal, invisible, I remember with gladness and thanksgiving all that Thou hast been to this world of men:

    Companion of the brave:
    Upholder of the loyal:
    Light of the wanderer:
    Joy of the pilgrim:
    Guide of the pioneer:
    Helper of labouring men:
    Refuge of the broken-hearted:
    Deliverer of the oppressed:
    Succour of the tempted:
    Strength of the victorious:
    Ruler of rulers:
    Friend of the poor:
    Rescuer of the perishing:
    Hope of the dying.

Give me faith now to believe that Thou canst be all in all to me, according to my need, if only I renounce all proud self-dependence and put my trust in Thee.

Forbid it, O Father, that the difficulty of living well should ever tempt me to fall into any kind of heedlessness or despair. May I keep it ever in mind that this human life was once divinely lived and this world once nobly overcome and this body of flesh, that now so sorely tries me, once made into Thy perfect dwelling-place.

Show thy lovingkindness to-night, O Lord, to all who stand in need of Thy help. Be with the weak to make them strong and with the strong to make them gentle. Cheer the lonely with Thy company and the distracted with Thy solitude. Prosper Thy Church in the fulfilment of her mighty task, and grant Thy blessing to all who have toiled to-day in Christ's name. Amen.

CREATOR Spirit, who broodest everlastingly over the lands and waters of earth, enduing them with forms and colours which no human skill can copy, give me to-day, I beseech Thee, the mind and heart to rejoice in Thy creation.

Forbid that I should walk through Thy beautiful world with unseeing eyes:

Forbid that the lure of the market-place should ever entirely steal my heart away from the love of the open acres and the green trees:

Forbid that under the low roof of workshop or office or study I should ever forget Thy great overarching sky:

Forbid that when all Thy creatures are greeting the morning with songs and shouts of joy, I alone should wear a dull and sullen face:

Let the energy and vigour which in Thy wisdom Thou hast infused into every living thing stir to-day within my being, that I may not be among Thy creatures as a sluggard and a drone:

And above all give me grace to use these beauties of earth without me and this eager stirring of life within me as means whereby my soul may rise from creature to Creator, and from nature to nature's God.

O Thou whose divine tenderness doth ever outsoar the narrow loves and charities of earth, grant me to-day a kind and gentle heart towards all things that live. Let me not ruthlessly hurt any creature of Thine. Let me take thought also for the welfare of little children, and of those who are sick, and of the poor; remembering that what I do unto the least of these His brethren I do unto Jesus Christ my Lord. Amen.

Aʟᴍɪɢʜᴛʏ and ever-blessed God, who hast not at any time left Thyself without witness among men, but hast in every age raised up saintly and prophetic spirits to lead us into the way of faith and love, I praise Thy name for the gift of Thy holy apostle, Saint Paul. I thank Thee for the zeal with which Thou didst endow him to carry to our western race that lamp of truth which Thou hadst lately lit in an eastern land.

Saint Paul said, *Let all bitterness, and wrath, and anger, and clamour, and evil speaking, be put away from you, with all malice: and be ye kind to one another, tender-hearted, forgiving one another, even as God for Christ's sake hath forgiven you.*

O God, incline my heart to follow in this way.

Saint Paul said, *Put ye on the Lord Jesus Christ, and make not provision for the flesh, to fulfil the lusts thereof.*

O God, incline my heart to follow in this way.

Saint Paul said, *I keep my body under, and bring it into subjection.*

O God, incline my heart to follow in this way.

Saint Paul said, *Let nothing be done through strife or vainglory; but in lowliness of mind let each esteem other better than themselves.*

O God, incline my heart to follow in this way.

Saint Paul said, *He that glorieth, let him glory in the Lord.*

O God, incline my heart to follow in this way.

Saint Paul said, *Continue in prayer, and watch in the same with thanksgiving: withal praying also for us, that God would open unto us a door of utterance, to speak the mystery of Christ.*

O God, I pray to-night especially for all who, following in the footsteps of Saint Paul, are now labouring to bring the light of Christ's gospel to foreign lands. Amen.

GETTING & KEEPING
HOLD (ON REALITY)

CONTRSTS

ALL Hail, O Lord my King! Reverently would I greet Thee at the beginning of another day! All praise and love and loyalty be unto Thee, O Lord most high!

Forbid, O Lord God, that my thoughts to-day should be wholly occupied with the world's passing show. Seeing that in Thy lovingkindness Thou hast given me the power to lift my mind to the contemplation of things unseen and eternal, forbid that I should remain content with the things of sense and time. Grant rather that each day may do something so to strengthen my hold upon the unseen world, so to increase my sense of its reality, and so to attach my heart to its holy interests that, as the end of my earthly life draws ever nearer, I may not grow to be a part of these fleeting earthly surroundings, but rather grow more and more conformed to the life of the world to come.

O Thou who seest and knowest all things, give me grace, I pray Thee, so to know Thee and so to see Thee that in knowing Thee I may know myself even as I am most perfectly known of Thee, and in seeing Thee may see myself as I verily am before Thee. Give me to-day some clear vision of my life in time as it appears to Thine eternity. Show me my own smallness and Thine infinite greatness. Show me my own sin and Thy perfect righteousness. Show me my own lovelessness and Thine exceeding love. Yet in Thy mercy show me also how, small as I am, I can take refuge in Thy greatness; how, sinful as I am, I may lean upon Thy righteousness; and how, loveless as I am, I may hide myself in Thy forgiving love. Cause my thoughts to dwell much to-day on the life and death of Jesus Christ my Lord, so that I may see all things in the light of the redemption which Thou hast granted to me in His name. Amen.

O THOU who art the Lord of the night as of the day and to whose will all the stars are obedient, in this hour of darkness I too would submit my will to Thine.

From the stirrings of self-will within my heart:
From cowardly avoidance of necessary duty:
From rebellious shrinking from necessary suffering:
From discontentment with my lot:
From jealousy of those whose lot is easier:
From thinking lightly of the one talent Thou hast
    given me, because Thou hast not given me five or
    ten:
From uncreaturely pride:
From undisciplined thought:
From unwillingness to learn and unreadiness to serve:
                O God, set me free.

O God my Father, who art often closest to me when I am farthest from Thee and who art near at hand even when I feel that Thou hast forsaken me, mercifully grant that the defeat of my self-will may be the triumph in me of Thine eternal purpose.

May I grow more sure of Thy reality and power:
May I attain a clearer mind as to the meaning of my
    life on earth:
May I strengthen my hold upon life eternal:
May I look more and more to things unseen:
May my desires grow less unruly and my imaginations
    more pure:
May my love for my fellow men grow deeper and
    more tender, and may I be more willing to take
    their burdens upon myself.

To thy care, O God, I commend my soul and the souls of all whom I love and who love me; through Jesus Christ our Lord. Amen.

H OLY, *Holy, Holy, Lord God Almighty; heaven and earth are full of Thy Glory; glory be to Thee, O Lord most high.*

O God, I crave Thy blessing upon this day of rest and refreshment. Let me rejoice to-day in Thy worship and find gladness in the singing of Thy praises. Forbid, I beseech Thee, that only my body should be refreshed to-day and not my spirit. Give me grace for such an act of self-recollection as may again bring together the scattered forces of my soul. Enable me to step aside for a little while from the busy life of common days and take thought about its meaning and its end. May Jesus Christ be to-day the companion of my thoughts, so that His divine manhood may more and more take root within my soul. May He be in me and I in Him, even as Thou wert in Him and through Him mayest be in me and I at rest in Thee.

O Thou who art the Source and Ground of all truth, Thou Light of lights, who hast opened the minds of men to discern the things that are, guide me to-day, I beseech Thee, in my hours of reading. Give me grace to choose the right books and to read them in the right way. Give me wisdom to abstain as well as to persevere. Let the Bible have proper place; and grant that as I read I may be alive to the stirrings of Thy Holy Spirit in my soul.

I pray, O God, for all human hearts that to-day are lifted up to Thee in earnest desire, and for every group of men and women who are met together to praise and magnify Thy name. Whatever be their mode of worship, be graciously pleased to accept their humble offices of prayer and praise, and lead them unto life eternal, through Jesus Christ our Lord. Amen.

H OLY Spirit of God, Thou who art a gracious and willing guest in every heart that is humble enough to receive Thee, be present now within my heart and guide my prayer. *— Thru Christ our Lord Amen.*

For all the gracious opportunities and privileges of this day, I give Thee thanks, O Lord:

For the rest I have this day enjoyed from the daily round of deeds:

For thine invitation to keep the day holy to Thyself:

For the house of prayer and the ministry of public worship:

For the blessed sacrament in which, as often as we eat and drink it, we remember our Lord's death and taste His living presence.

For all the earthly symbols by which heavenly realities have to-day laid firmer hold upon my soul:

For the books I have read and the music which has uplifted me:

For this day's friendly intercourse:

For the Sabbath peace of Christian homes:

For the interior peace that has ruled within my heart.

Grant, O heavenly Father, that the spiritual refreshment I have this day enjoyed may not be left behind and forgotten as to-morrow I return to the cycle of common tasks. Here is a fountain of inward strength. Here is a purifying wind that must blow through all my business and all my pleasures. Here is light to enlighten all my road. Therefore, O God, do Thou enable me so to discipline my will that in hours of stress I may honestly seek after those things for which I have prayed in hours of peace.

Ere I lie down to sleep, I commit all my dear ones to Thine unsleeping care; through Jesus Christ our Lord. Amen.